Let's Hear It For

# Labrador Retrievers

Written by

**Piper Welsh**

Scan for Related Titles and Teacher Resources

www.rourkeeducationalmedia.com

PHOTO CREDITS: Cover: © Bonzami Emmanuelle; page 4: © Daniela Jakob; page 5: © Eric IsselÃƒÂ©e; page 6: © Ali Peterson; page 7: © Walter Arce; page 8: © Roland IJdema; page 9: © Emir Simsek; page 10: © Zuzana Buránová; page 11: © Walter Arce; page 12: © V. J. Matthew; page 13: © JoeGough; page 14: © Karen Town; page 15: © agurovic; page 16: © John McAllister (German Shorthaired Pointer), © Erik Lam (Irish Setter, English Setter); page 17: © Michael Roberts; page 18: © Elena Elisseeva; page 19: © Kampee Patisena; page 20: © Bonzami Emmanuelle; page 21: © Jeffrey Banke; page 22: © Erik Lam

Edited by: Luana Mitten

Cover design by: Renee Brady
Interior design by: Ashley Morgan

**Library of Congress PCN Data**

Welsh, Piper.
Let's Hear It For Labrador Retrievers / Piper Welsh.
p. cm. -- (Dog Applause)
Includes index.
ISBN 978-1-62169-865-4 (hardcover)
ISBN 978-1-62169-760-2 (softcover)
ISBN 978-1-62169-966-8 (e-Book)
Library of Congress Control Number: 2013936476

**Also Available as:**

Rourke Educational Media
Printed in the United States of America,
North Mankato, Minnesota

rourkeeducationalmedia.com
customerservice@rourkeeducationalmedia.com • PO Box 643328 Vero Beach, Florida 32964

# Table of Contents

***Labradors are fun-loving, athletic dogs.***

# Labrador Retrievers

Labrador Retrievers are big, gentle dogs with great **instincts** to retrieve. Retrieving dogs are especially good at being trained to bring objects back to their owners.

Many Labradors were used as bird hunting dogs because of this excellent retrieving instinct. But Labradors make fantastic companion dogs too.

## Labrador Retriever Facts

| | |
|---|---|
| **Weight:** | 55-80 pounds (25-36 kilograms) |
| **Height:** | 21.5-24.5 inches (55-62 centimeters) |
| **Country of Origin:** | Canada |
| **Life Span:** | 12-13 years |

Labrador Retrievers are easily the most popular **purebred** dogs in both the United States and Canada. American Kennel Club (AKC) records show that Labs took the number one position in 1991. They continue to hold it into the new century and they are still the number one breed today.

***Many people describe the Labrador's personality as "easy going," meaning that most things do not upset them.***

# Look at Me!

Labs have short, straight coats over dense undercoats. The undercoat keeps them warm in most weather conditions.

The early Labs were black. In more recent years, **breeders** have developed yellow and chocolate Labs, too.

Labs have broad heads with floppy ears and strong, fairly square jaws. Their tails are long and straight, and rounded like a flagpole.

***If there's water you can usually count on playtime for a Labrador. In general, Labs love to splash and swim.***

***Young Labradors can have lots of energy so it is important that owners give them plenty of time to exercise.***

# History of the Labrador

Labrador is a large territory in eastern Canada. One can certainly find Labrador Retrievers there. But the first Labs were from Newfoundland. Newfoundland is a province in cold, foggy northeastern Canada.

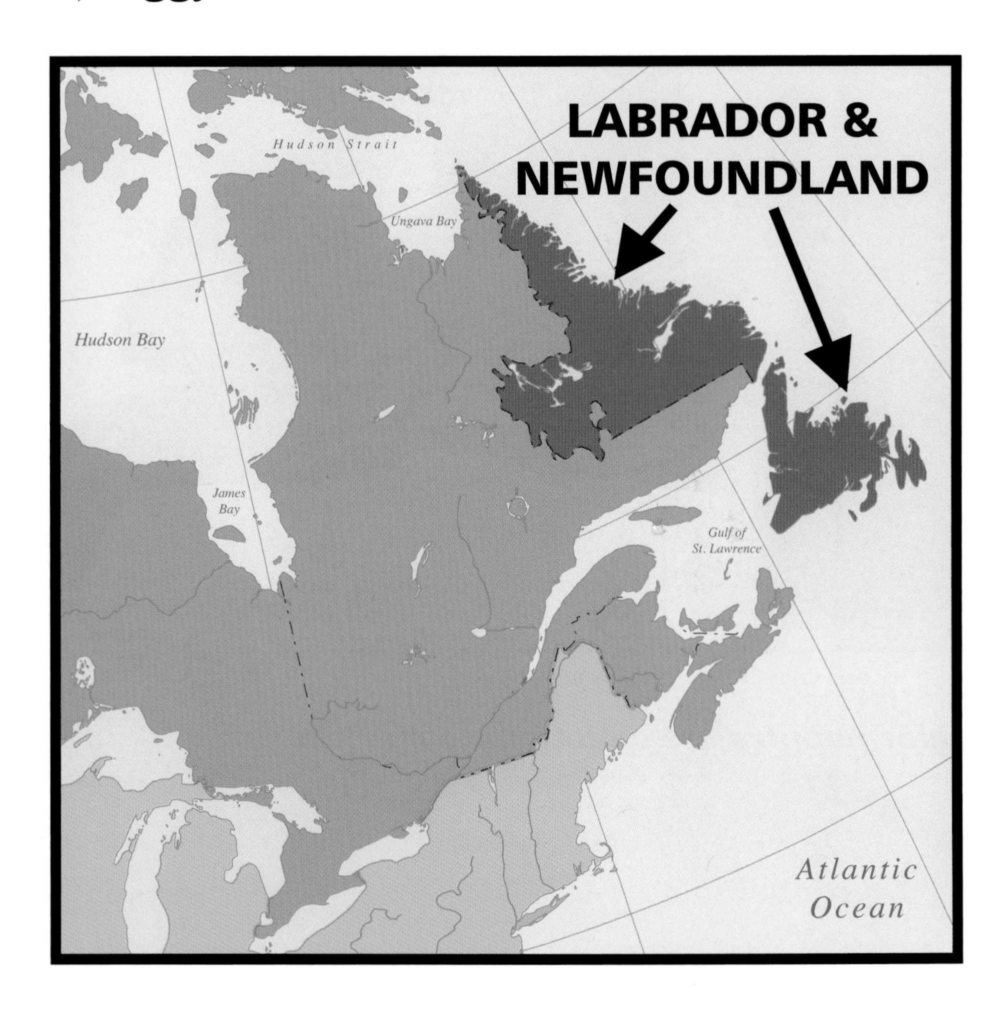

With their dense, black coats, the first Lab-like retrievers were true water dogs. They retrieved ducks, geese, and even fish. They also pulled small fishing boats in icy water.

***Labrador puppies are affectionate and playful.***

***Labradors respond quickly in the field. This quality makes them prized sporting dogs.***

These dogs of the early 1800s were called St. John's Newfoundland dogs. St. John's is the largest city in Newfoundland. Curiously, dogs of this type began to die out. One reason was a costly dog tax in Newfoundland.

Many of the St. John's Newfoundlands, however, had been taken to England in the early 1800s. English dog breeders **mated** some of their Newfoundlands with other retrievers. Over many years, the result of their work was the modern, water-loving Labrador Retriever.

***In Newfoundland, Canada, people are proud of their role in the development of two fine canine breeds, the Labrador and the Newfoundland.***

*Labradors will retrieve and carry just about anything. So, if you are thinking about owning a Lab, be ready to play.*

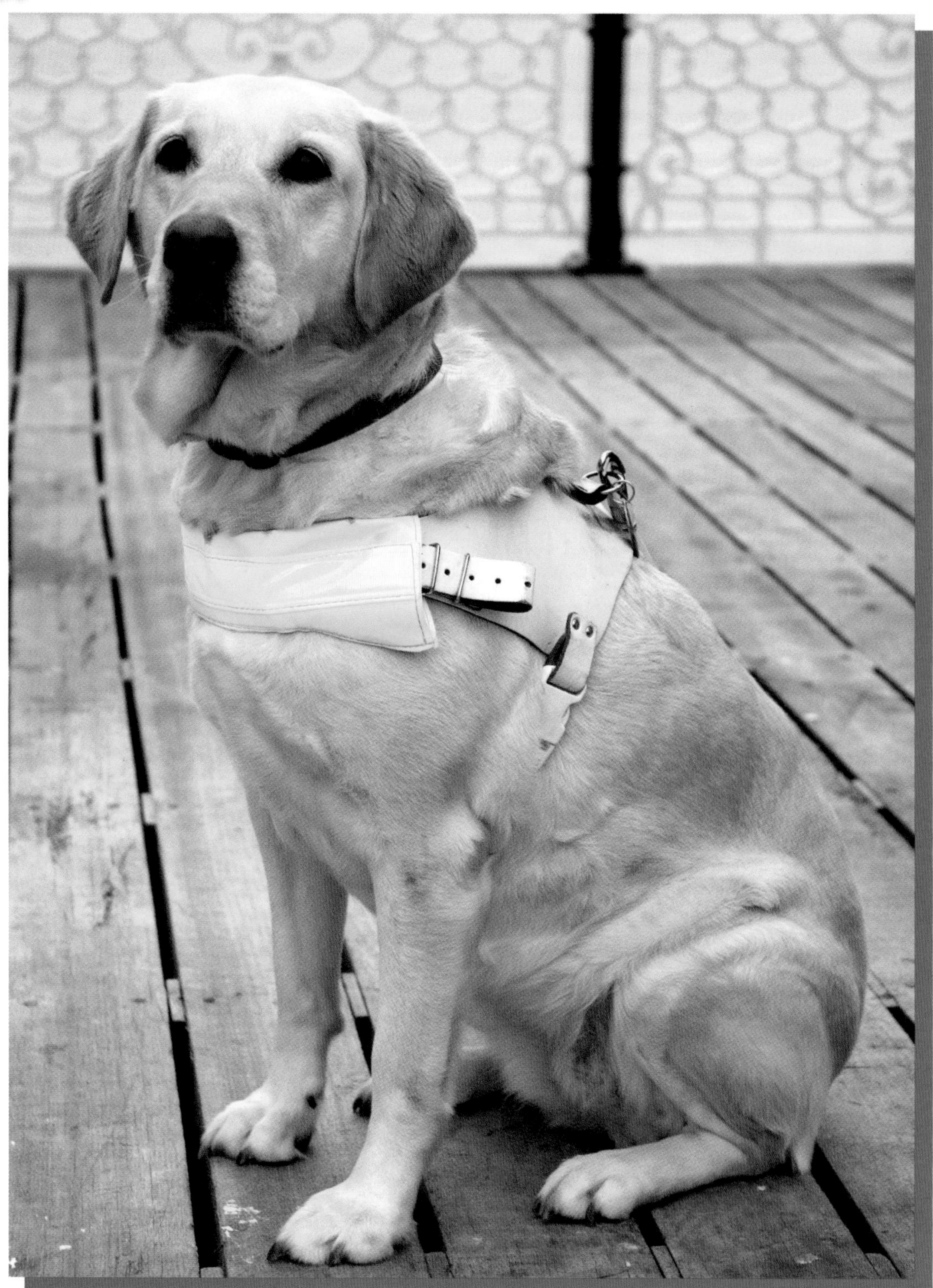

***Labs make excellent service dogs because of their desire to work with and please people. After years of training, they make reliable, gentle service animals.***

# The Perfect Service Dog

Labs are one of just three dog **breeds** commonly used as guide, or service, dogs for people who are blind. These dogs undergo almost two years of training at special schools. Then they can begin work with their masters who are visually impaired. Other Labs are trained to work with people who have other **disabilities**, such as epilepsy.

***As service dogs, Labradors must be trained to be watchful, calm, and responsible. They have to be able to focus on their human companion, not other distracting dogs.***

Labs are also used as search and rescue dogs. Some worked at the World Trade Center disaster in New York City in 2001. Labs are most popular, though, as family companions.

Labs are one breed in the group of sporting, or gun, dogs. Hunters use hard-working Labs to retrieve many kinds of game birds, especially ducks and geese.

***There are many other breeds of dogs in the sporting group.***

# Perfect Companions

Good Labs are wonderful companions for children or adults. They are quick to learn, **obedient**, good-natured, and trusting. They are comfortable with strangers and other pets.

***Labs are some of the most popular pets in the United States because they are patient with children and other animals.***

***If you have a swimming pool, you might want to doggy proof it or you are sure to find your Lab in it every chance he gets.***

Indoors, Labs are usually calm and not quick to bark unless startled. Outdoors, Labs love to run, swim, and, of course, retrieve. Labs are all around athletes.

Labs do very well in obedience trials. Obedience trials test how well a dog has learned to follow human commands. In field obedience trials, Labs show their skills at retrieving birds or following a scent.

Some Lab owners enter their dogs in **conformation** shows. Conformation shows judge how well a dog meets the ideal shape and structure of its breed.

Many people in the United States and Canada would agree, Labradors are some of the most versatile and delightful dogs in the world.

***For agility competitions, dogs must zip and zoom over obstacles as their human gives them directions on where to go.***

***Dock diving is a popular competition for Labradors. Dogs must leap off of a dock to retrieve a toy. The dog with the longest jump into the water is the winner.***

# Doggie Advice

Puppies are cute and cuddly, but buying one should never be done without serious thought. Choosing the right breed of dog requires some homework. And remember that a dog will require more than love and great patience. It will require food, exercise, grooming, a warm, safe place to live, and medical care.

A dog can be your best friend, but you need to be its best friend, too. For more information about buying and owning a dog, contact the American Kennel Club at *www.akc.org/index.cfm* or the Canadian Kennel Club at *www.ckc.ca*.

# Glossary

**breeders** (BREE-duhrz): people who raise animals, such as dogs, and carefully choose the mothers and fathers for more dogs

**breeds** (BREEDZ): particular kinds of domestic animals within a larger group, such as the Labrador Retriever breed within the dog group

**conformation** (con-fohr-MAY-shun): the desired form and structure of an animal based on its breed

**disabilities** (dis-eh-BIL-eh-teez): losses of abilities, such as deafness being the loss of hearing ability

**instincts** (IN-stinktz): actions or behaviors with which an animal is born, rather than learned behaviors

**mated** (MAY-tud): to have been paired with another dog for the purpose of having pups

**obedient** (oh-BEE-dee-ent): showing the ability to follow directions or commands

**purebred** (PYOOR-bred): an animal of a single (pure) breed

# Index



## Websites to Visit

www.akc.org/breeds
www.vetstreet.com/dogs/breeds#sporting
www.dogbreedinfo.com/labrador.htm

## Show What You Know

1. What things are Labrador Retrievers good for besides being a pet?
2. What color coat can a Labrador Retriever have?
3. Where were the first Labrador Retrievers from?